This book belongs to:

Draw & Color
Fruit

Coloring Book
Mary Lou Brown & Sandy Mahony

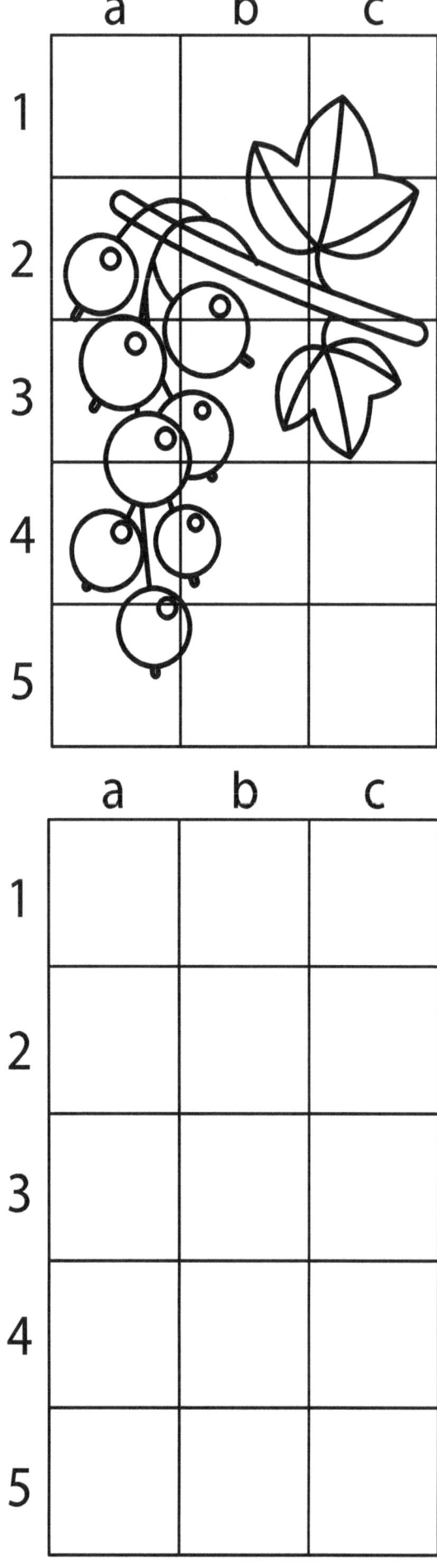

Red Currants

	a	b	c
1			
2			
3			
4			
5			

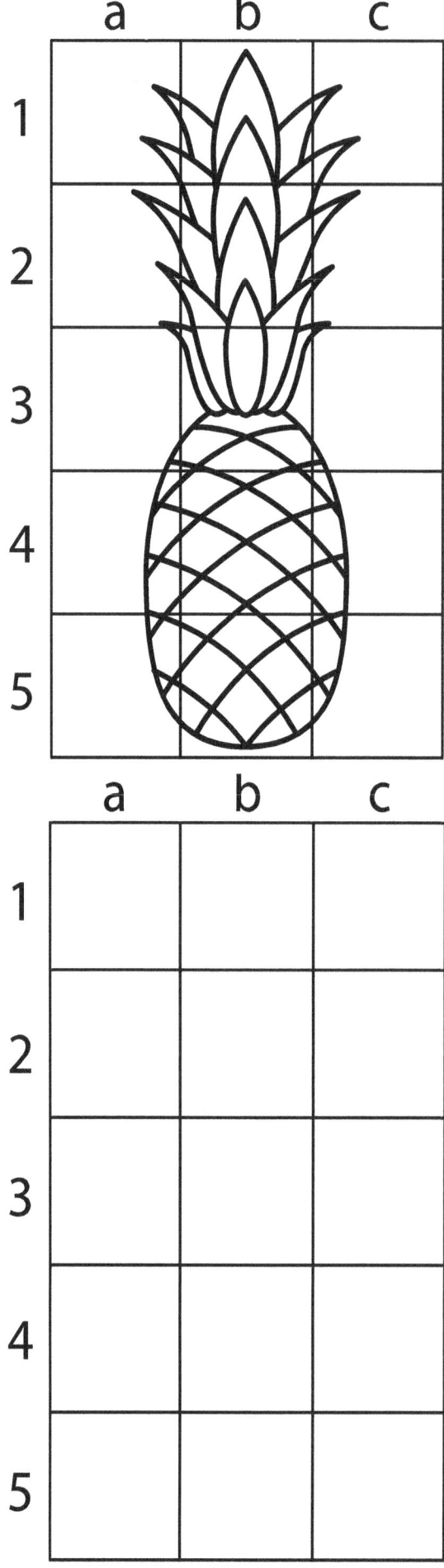

	a	b	c
1			
2			
3			
4			
5			

Pineapple

	a	b	c
1			
2			
3			
4			
5			

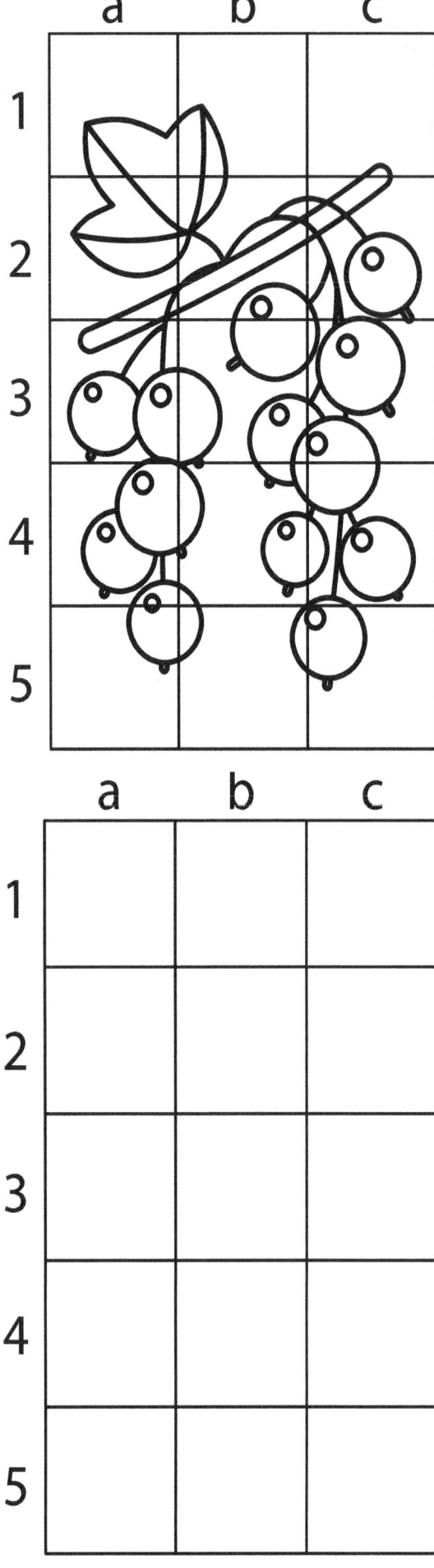

	a	b	c
1			
2			
3			
4			
5			

Black Currants

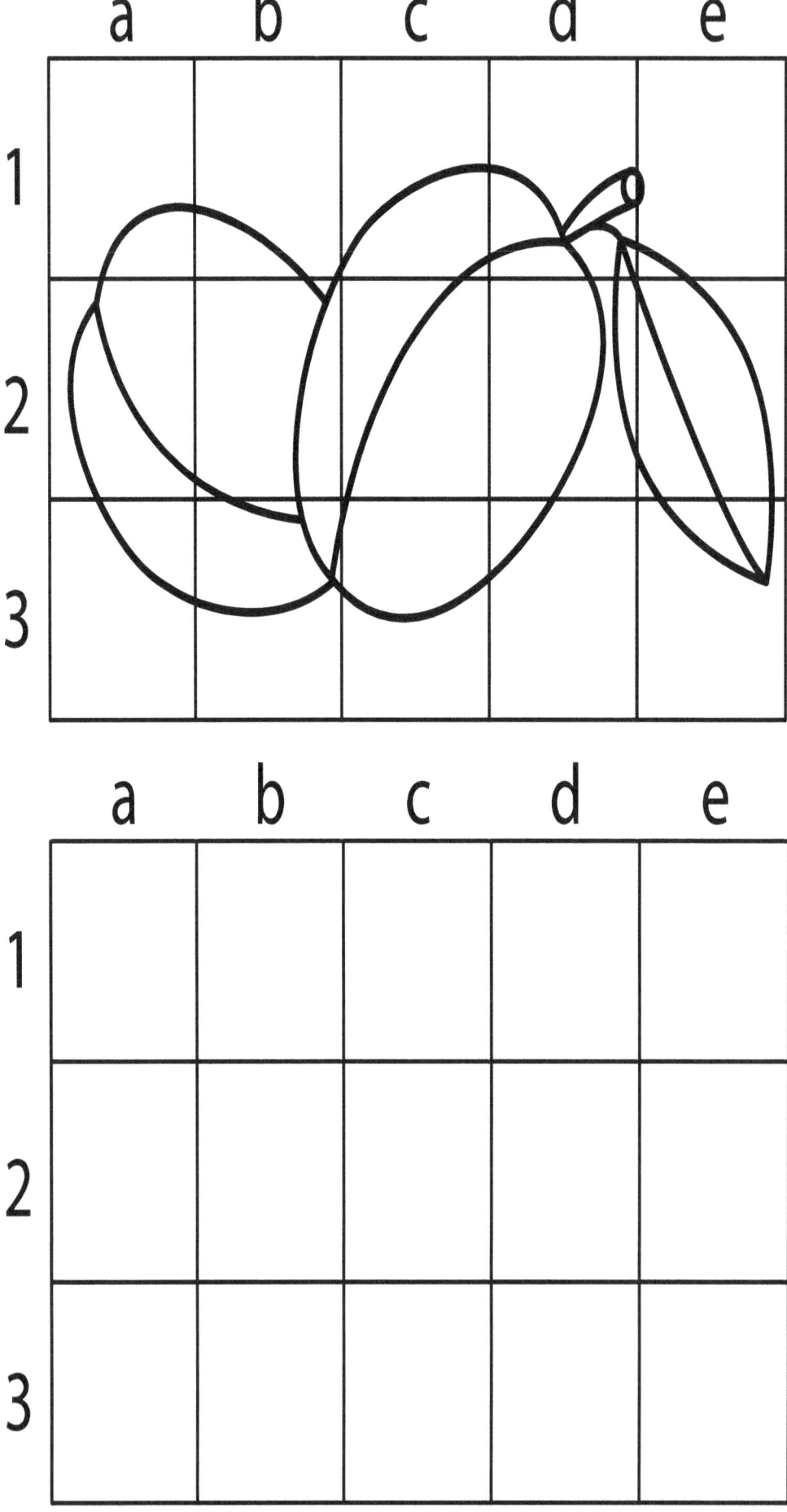

Plums

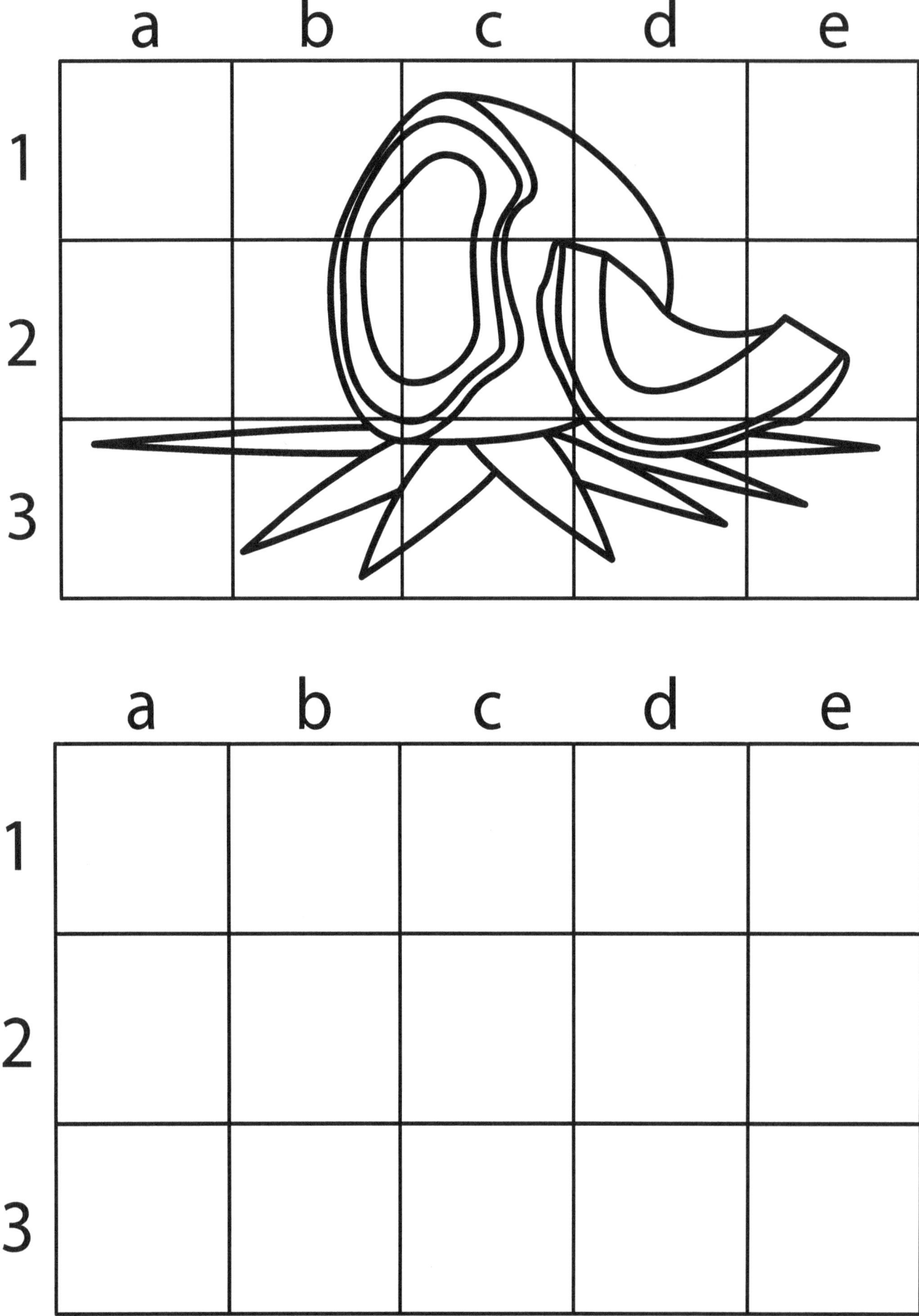

Coconut

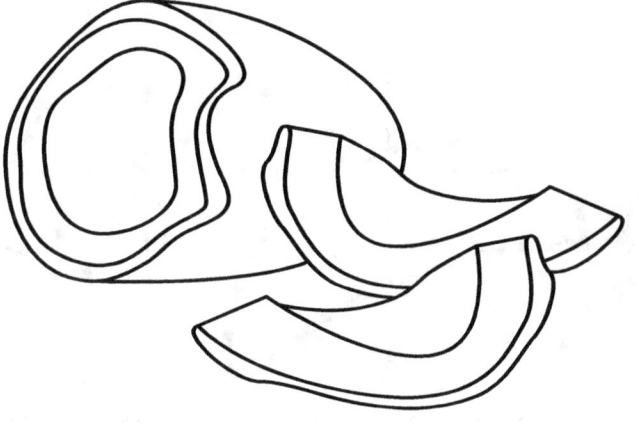

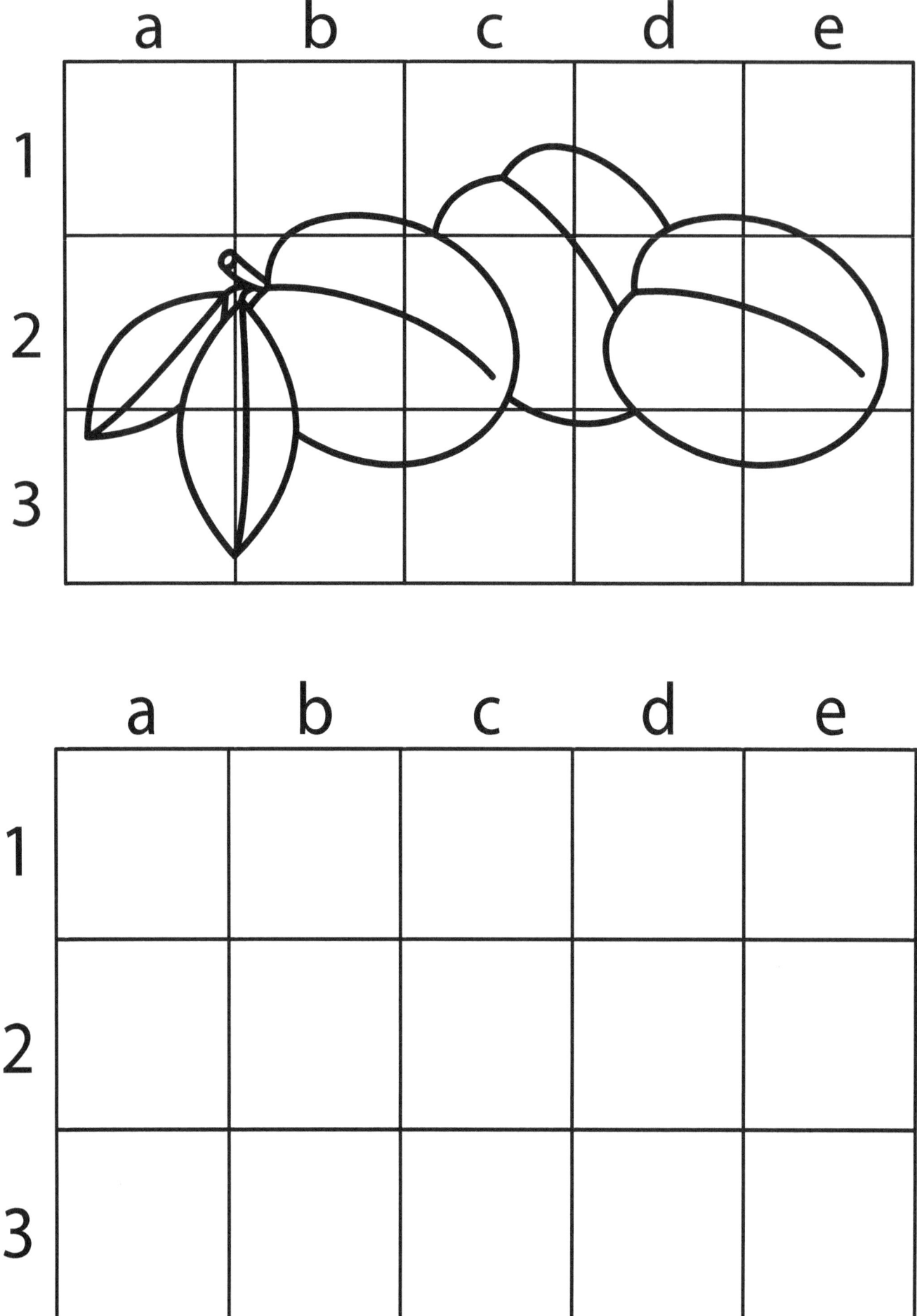

Apricots

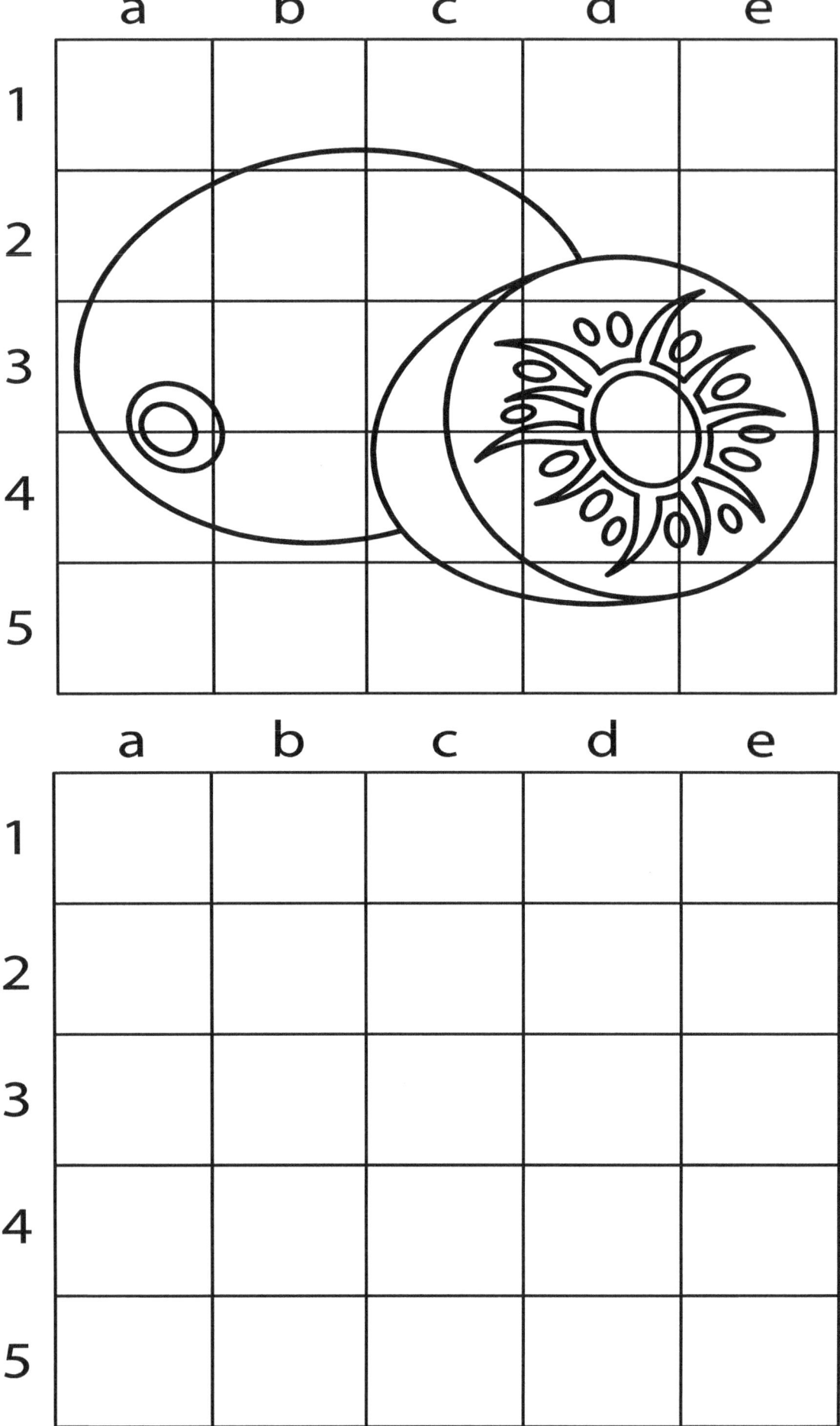

Kiwi

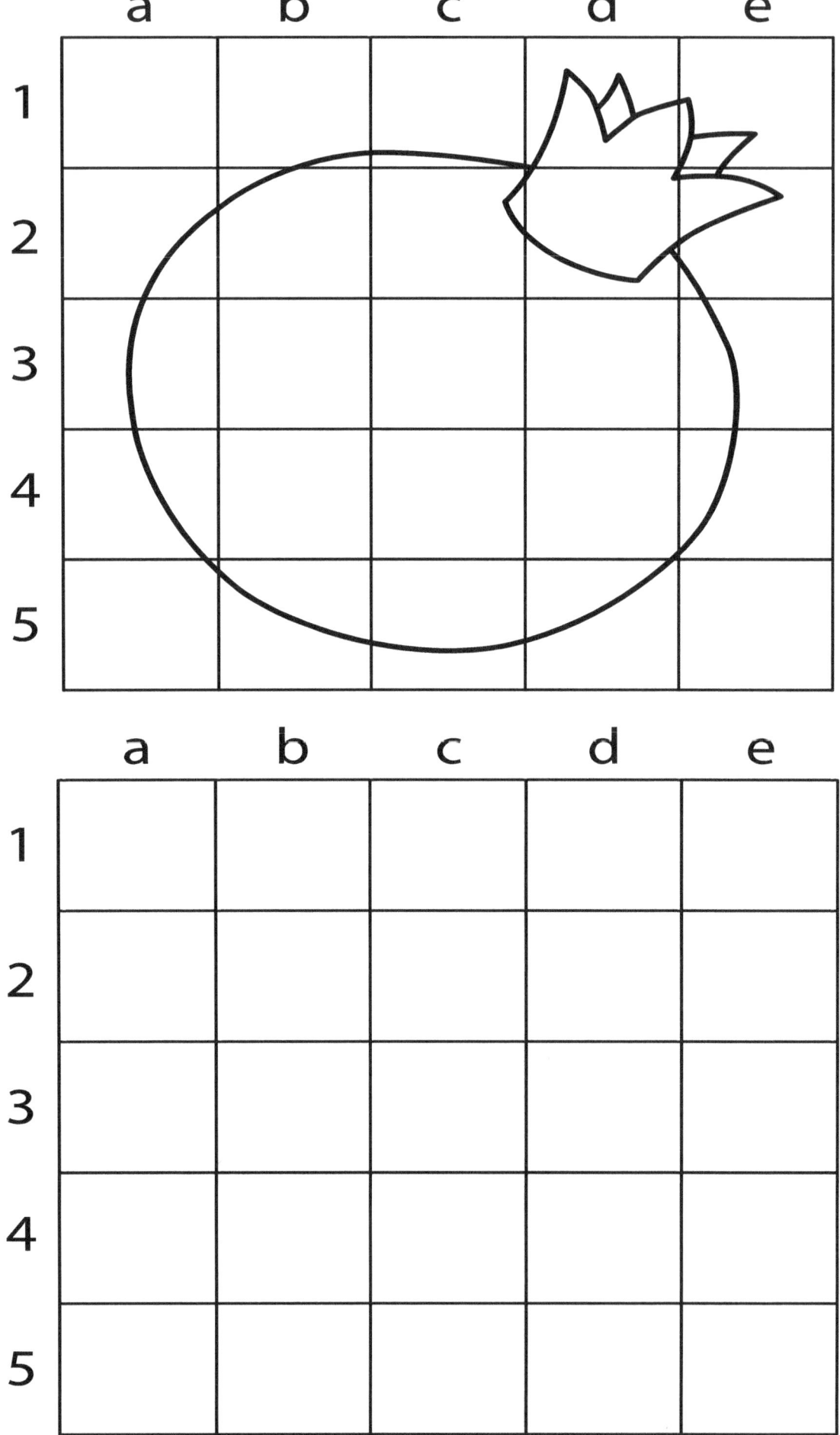

Pomegranate

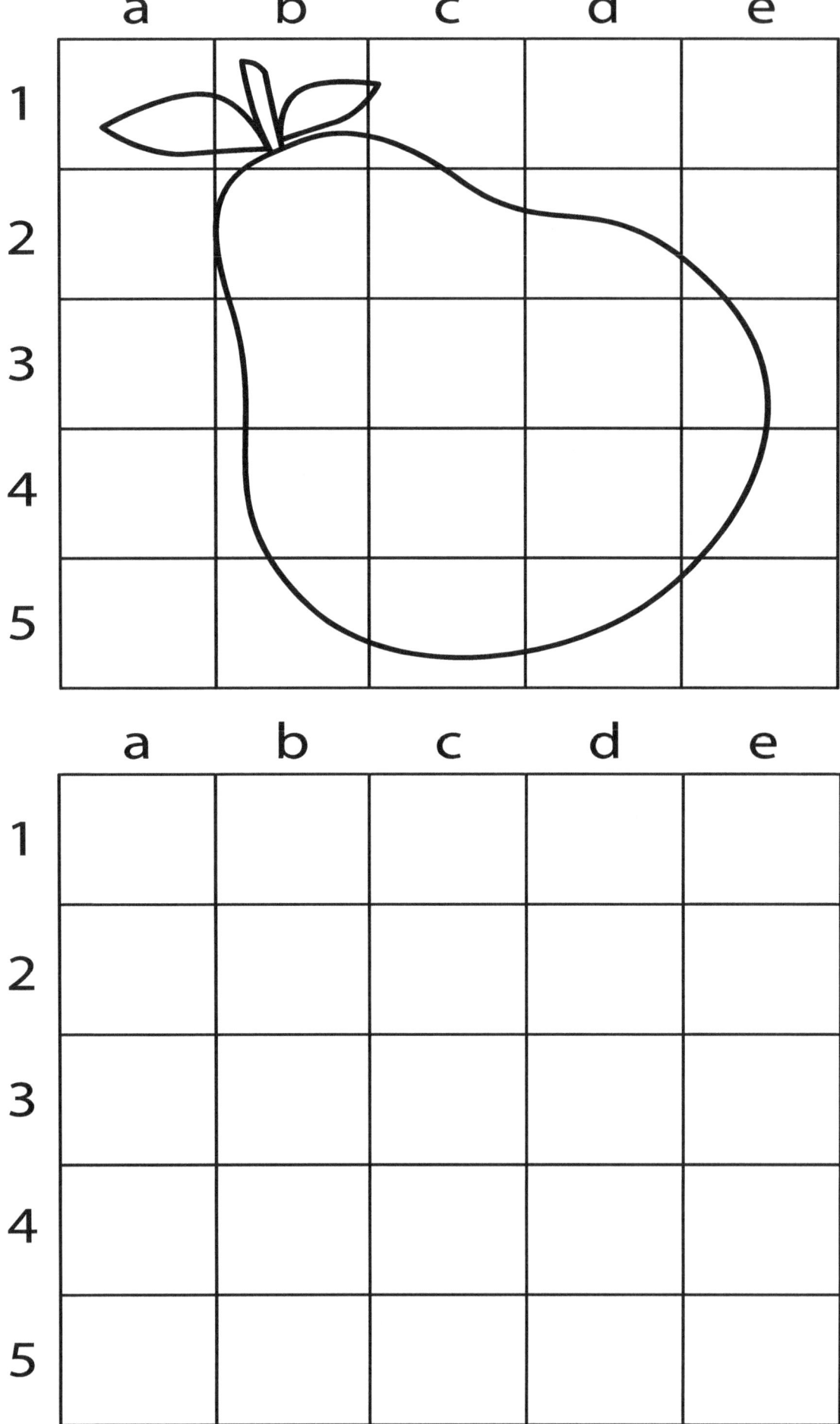

Pear

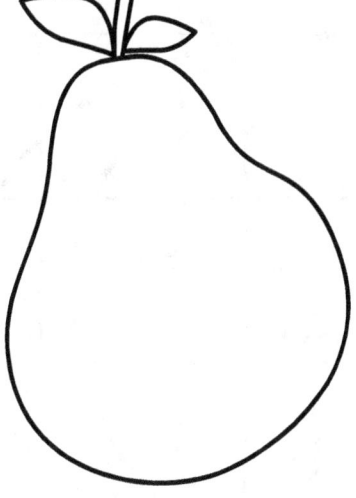

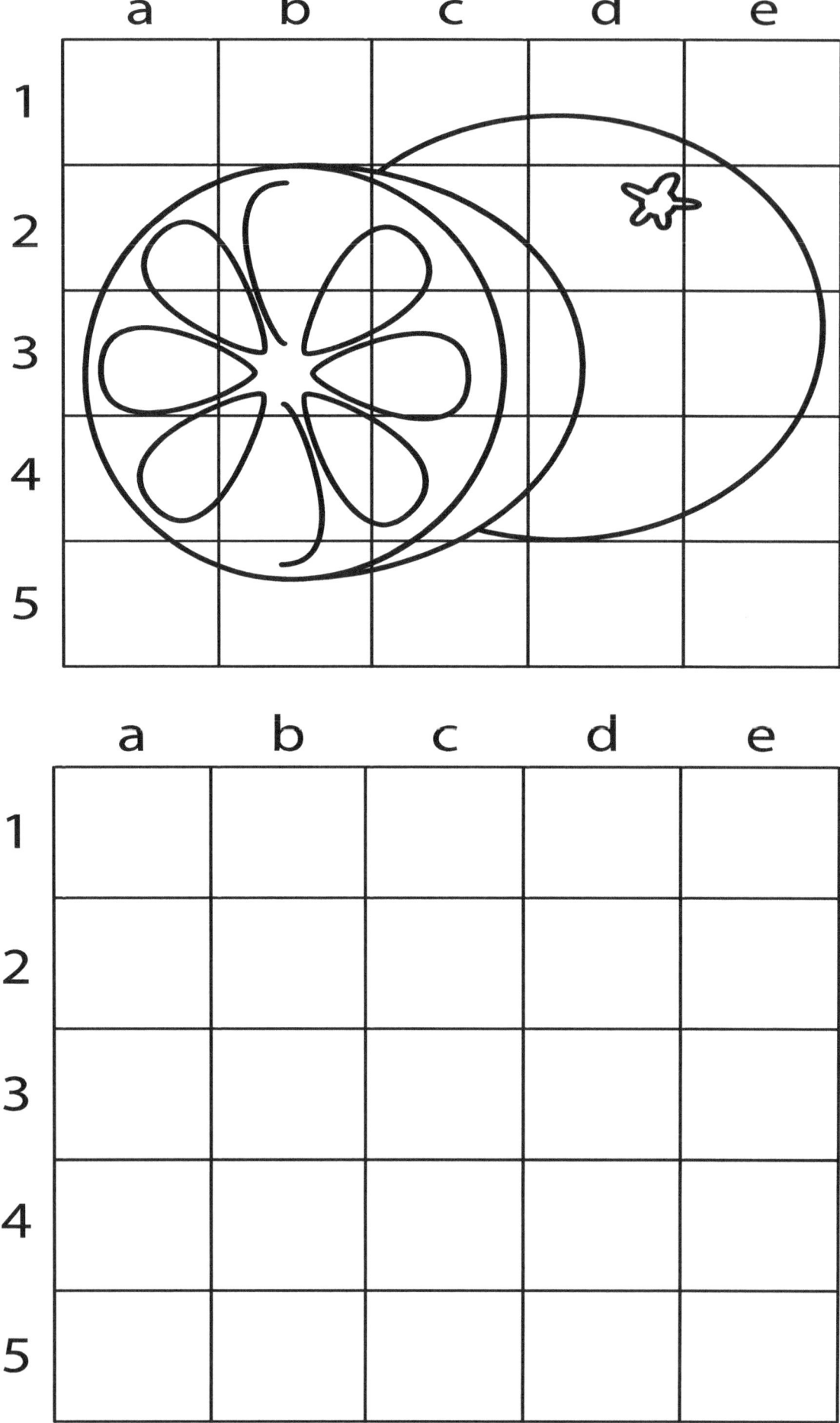

Orange

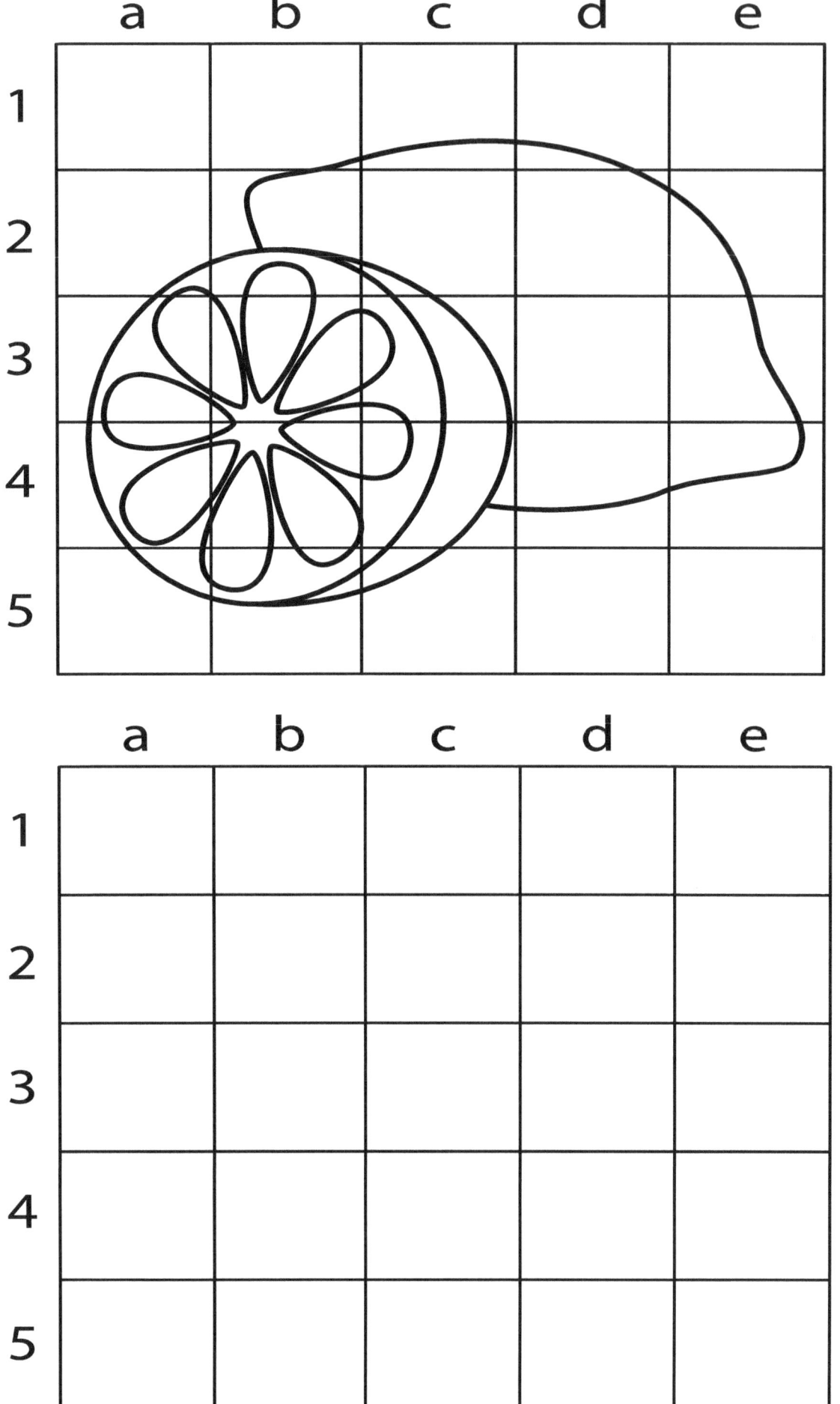

Lemon

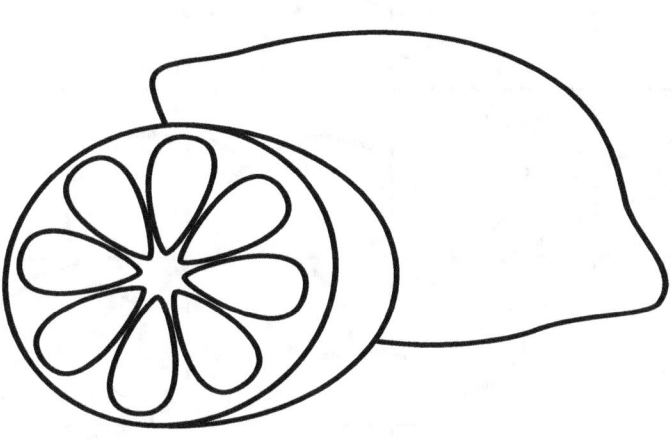

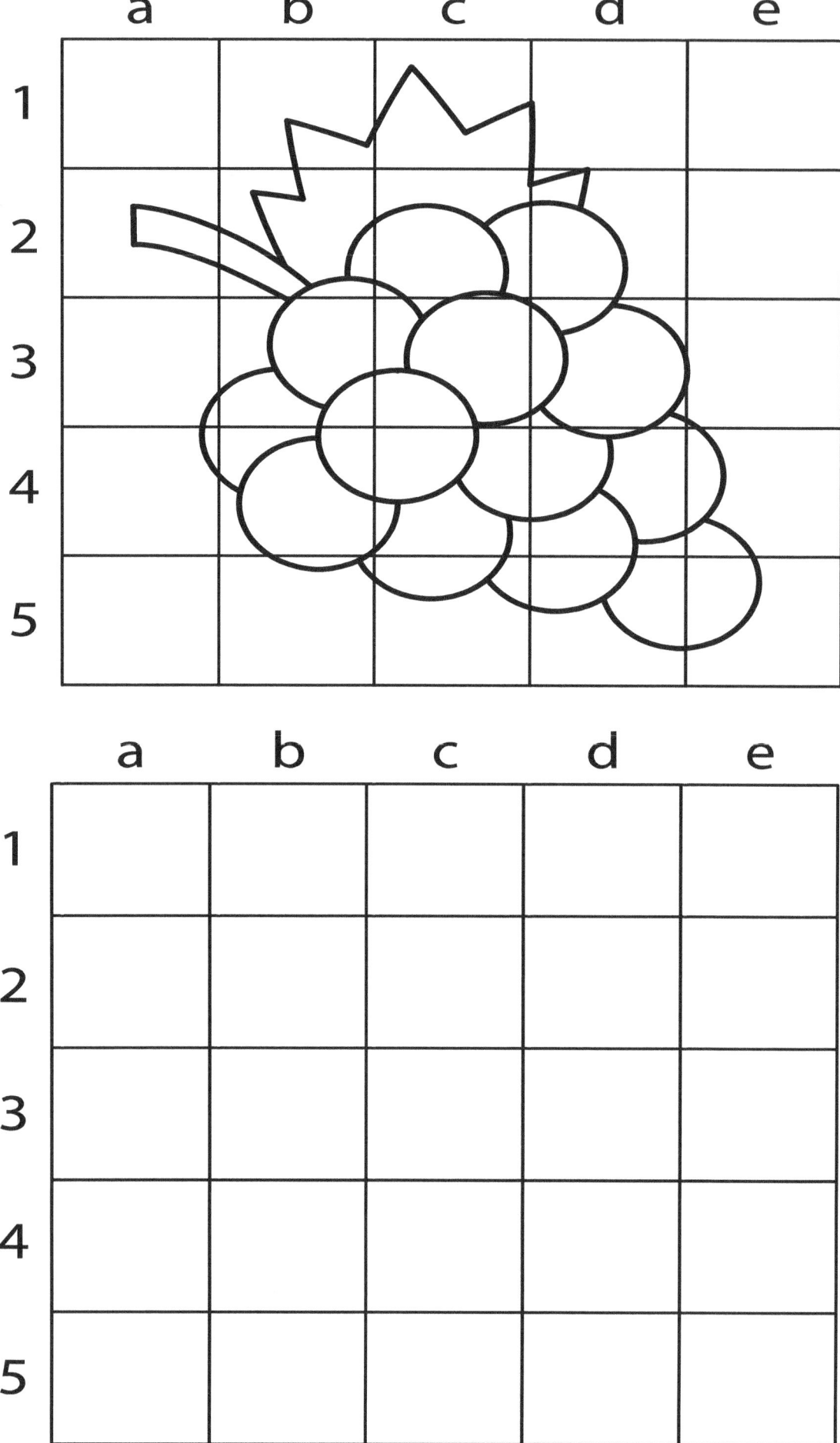

Grapes

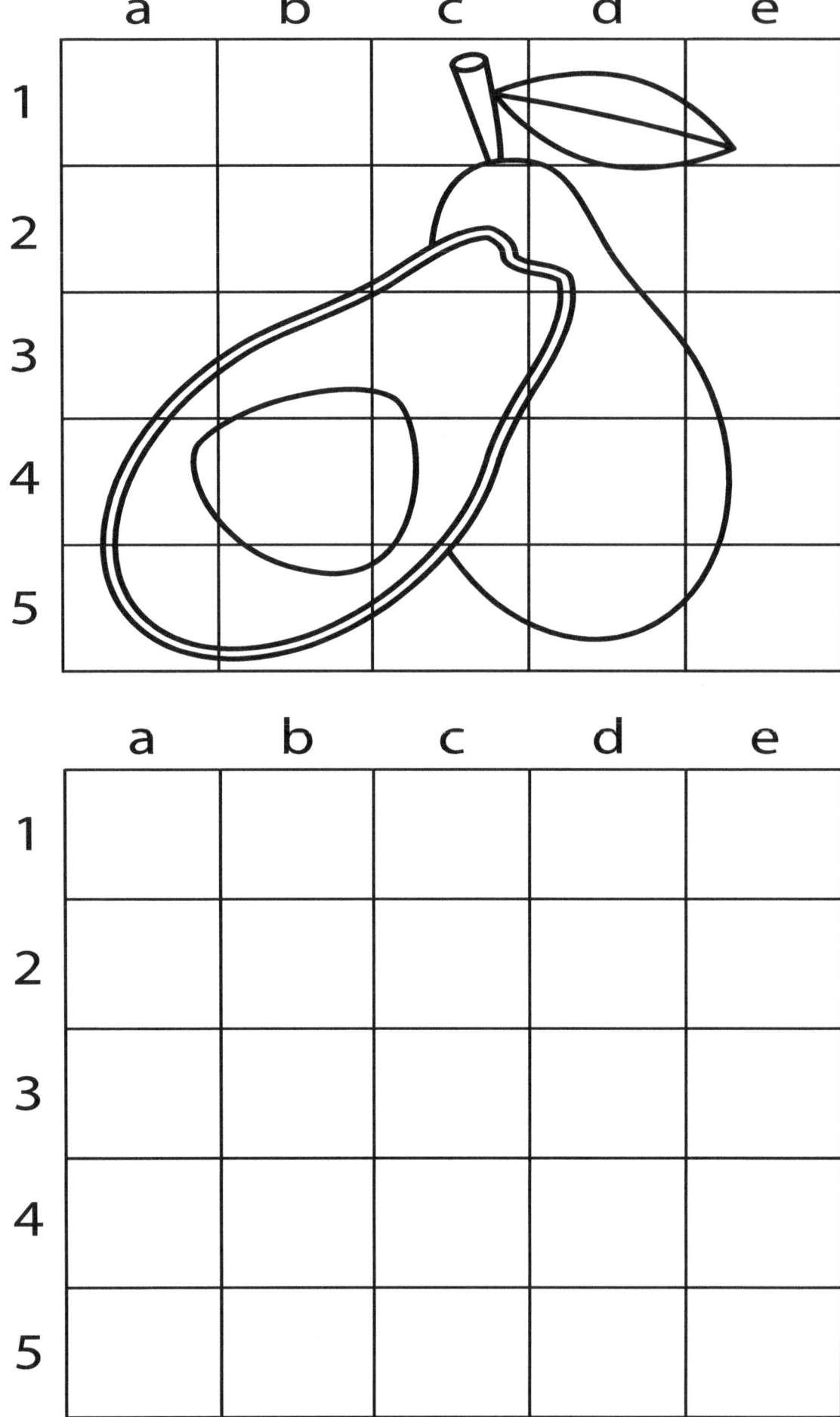

Avocados

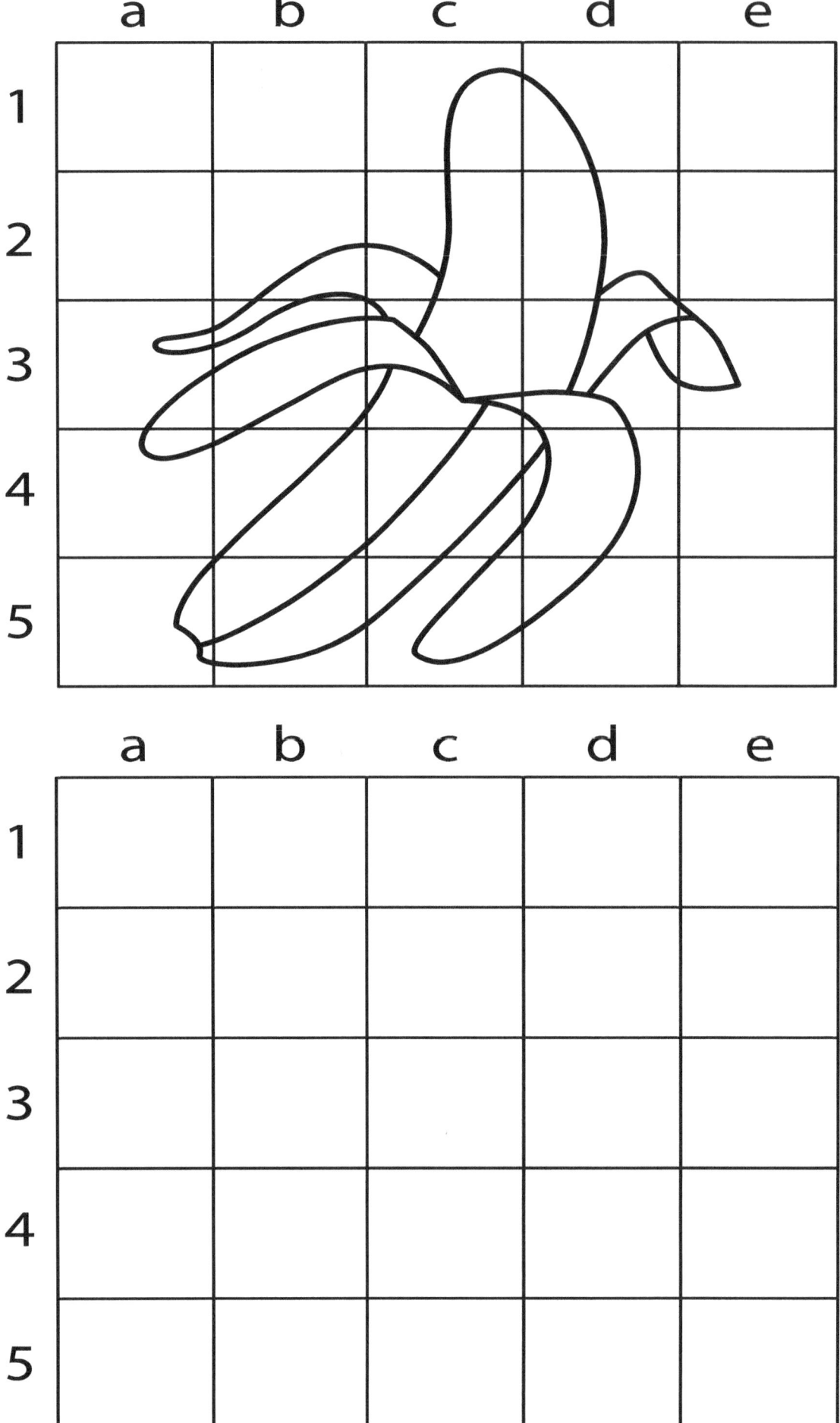

Banana

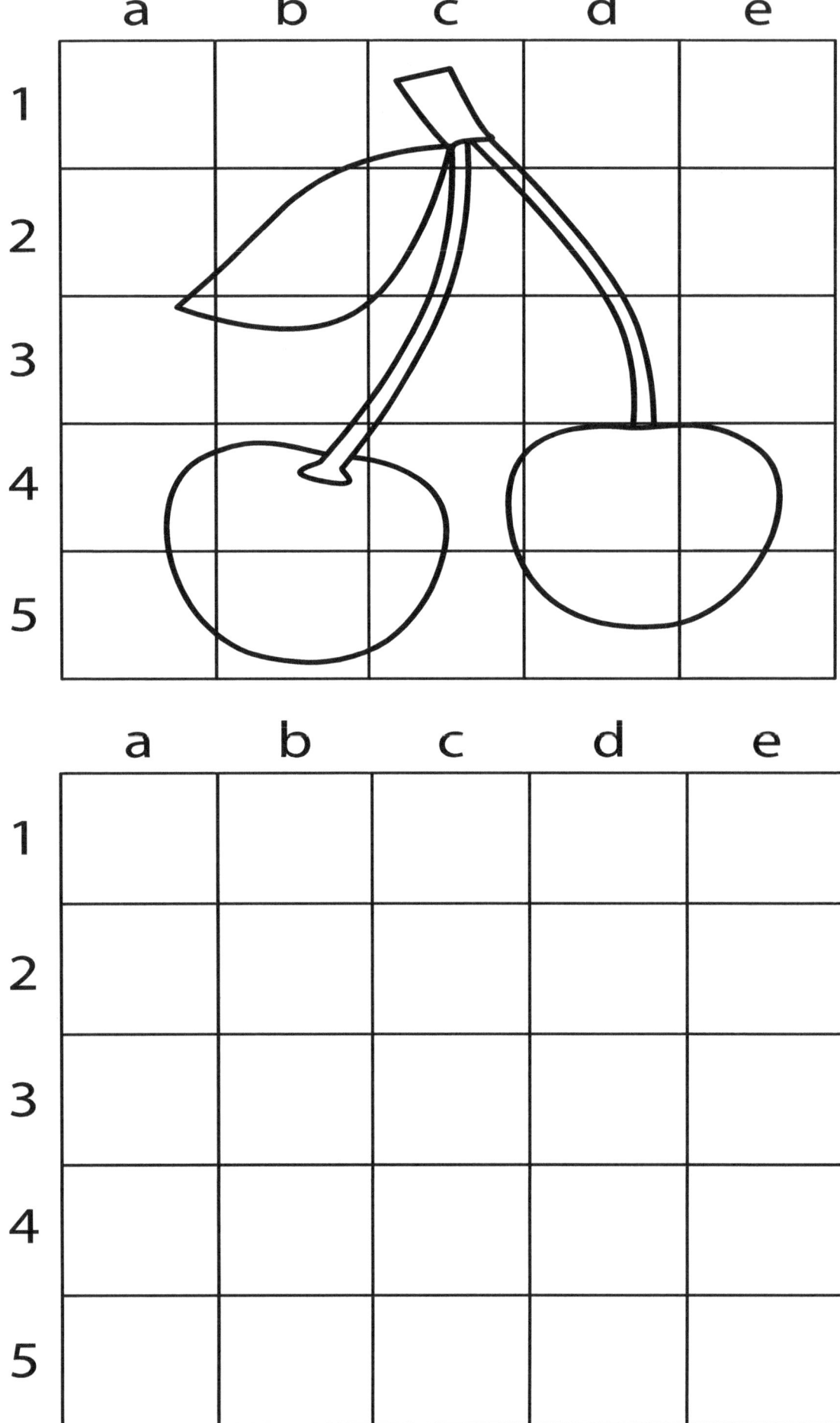

Cherries

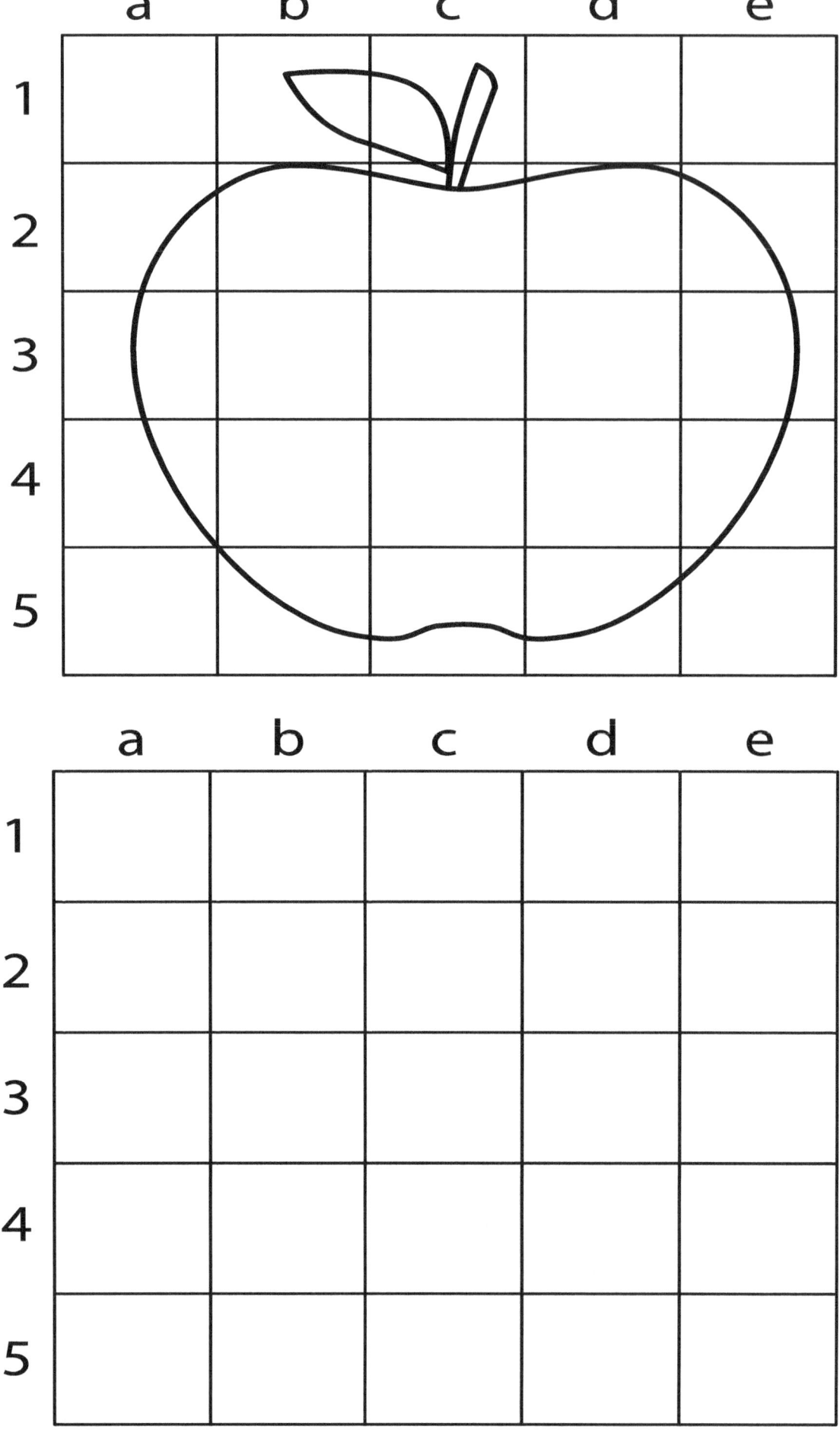

Apple

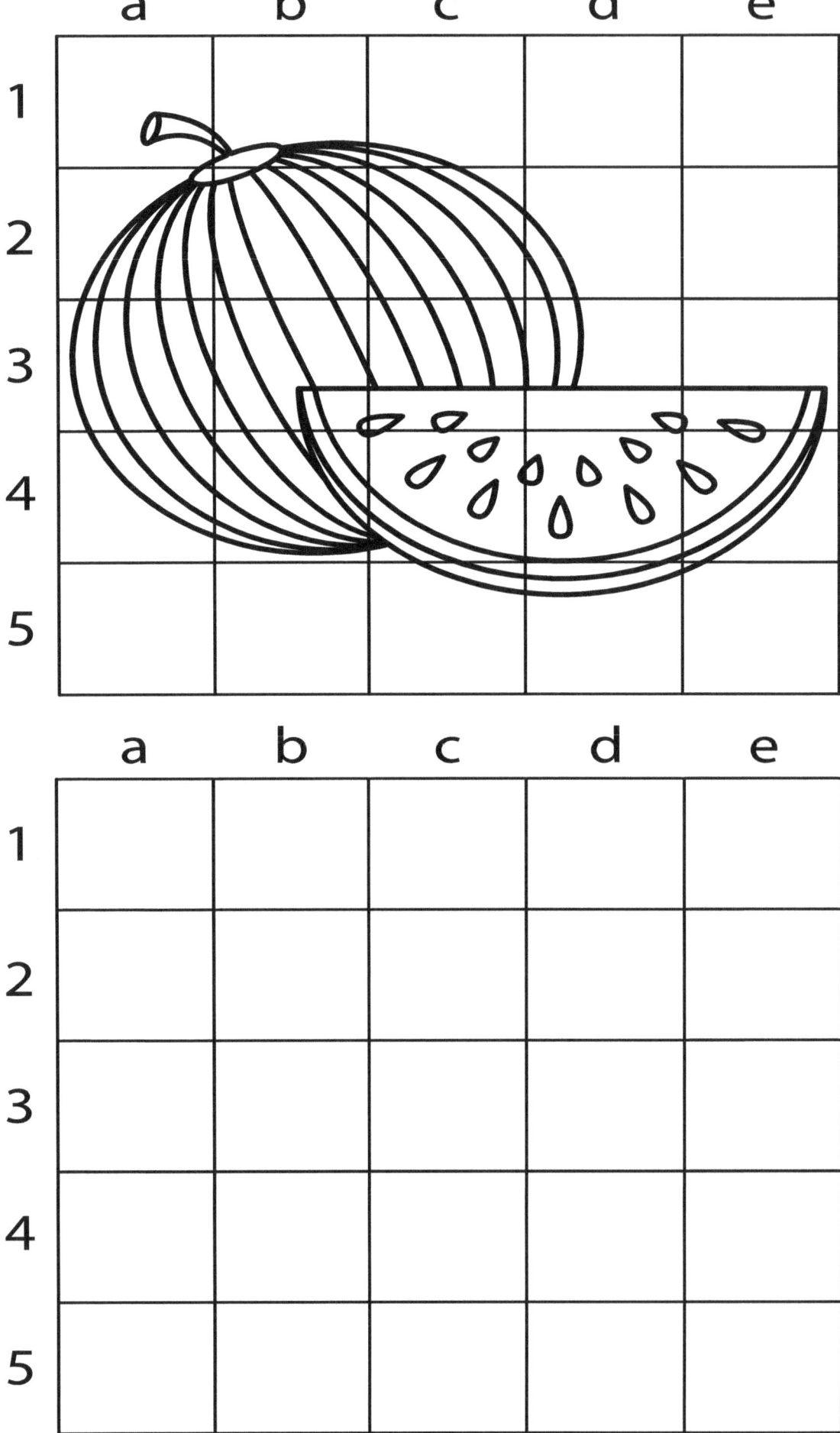

Watermelon

adventurelearningpress.com

www.ingramcontent.com/pod-product-compliance
Lightning Source LLC
Chambersburg PA
CBHW081802280526
45789CB00008B/2960